Parish Nativity Play

— KEVIN CAREY —

Sacristy Press

Sacristy Press
PO Box 612, Durham, DH1 9HT

www.sacristy.co.uk

First published in 2016 by Sacristy Press, Durham

Copyright © Kevin Carey 2016
The moral rights of the author have been asserted

All rights reserved, no part of this publication may be reproduced or transmitted in any form or by any means, electronic, mechanical photocopying, documentary, film or in any other format without prior written permission of the publisher.

Sacristy Limited, registered in England & Wales, number 7565667

British Library Cataloguing-in-Publication Data
A catalogue record for the book is available from the British Library

Paperback ISBN 978-1-910519-40-0
Hardback ISBN 978-1-910519-41-7

For the "Growing Together" house-group, without which this Play would not have been completed.

PREFACE

From a Christian standpoint, of the four major events in human history—the beginning and end of creation (or, as we might more broadly term it, time), and the Incarnation and the Resurrection of Jesus—the event about which we know least is the Incarnation. Science is still groping for a full understanding of the birth and death of time but at least it has created an elegant paradigm. By contrast, there are four different accounts of the Crucifixion, death and Resurrection of Jesus by the four Evangelists and only two of them have anything to say about the Incarnation and, even then, their narratives hardly coincide.

There being such little scriptural material, a serious play about the Incarnation must do what it can to marry the two accounts, supplemented by imagination.

My major points of departure from tradition, and the areas where I have taken the greatest liberty—or, to put it another way, have exercised the greatest imagination to achieve coherence—are in the scenes which involve the wise men. Matthew, somewhat confusingly, reflecting his penchant for duplicates—notably the two donkeys in 21.1-7—says successively in verses 2.1 and 2.2 that the wise men came from the east, saw a star in the east and then followed it to the east. If they travelled towards the star they must have come from west of it, which is the line I have taken by beginning their final journey in Alexandria, where they congregate to make their preparations. Using this device, the men could still have come from the east. Seeing the "star" moving from west to east, "ahead of them . . . until it stopped over the place where the child was" (Matthew 2.9), when the men are either travelling south from Jerusalem to Bethlehem or, in the alternative scenario, travelling north to Nazareth, makes no sense.

All one can do is to get as close to the meaning as possible.

I have presented two theories to account for "the star": one being a planetary conjunction; the other a comet, allowing the wise men to debate the issue. However, as the drama takes place in a miraculous ecology, anything is possible.

There is a long tradition, in contradiction of the popular crib and a great deal of Renaissance art, that these men did not visit Jesus in Bethlehem, in spite of Matthew 2.8–9, but went instead to Nazareth to worship a child perhaps two years of age. The explanation for this is the use of "house" (as opposed to the traditional "stable") in Matthew 2.11. Joseph would hardly resort to a public inn out of desperation in the town of his tribe as if he had no relations there.

This naturally leads to my second departure from tradition: I understand the Greek word *kataluma* in Luke 2.7 to mean a "residence", as it does in Luke 22.11, rather than "inn" which is more usually represented by the Greek *pandocheion*. Consistent with the narrative of the town of Bethlehem being unusually over-populated because of tax registration, I surmise that the spare room of Joseph's relative was full, so the young couple were given space in the lower part of the house where the animals were kept at night and so, after the birth, Mary wrapped Jesus in bands of cloth and laid him in the most comfortable place she could find, in the hay-filled animal feeding trough. This, in turn, makes the visit of the wise men to a domestic environment, rather than a stable out-house or a house in Nazareth, much more credible; the price we pay is the loss of the villainous innkeeper and the pathos surrounding the birth of an outcast in an out-house—but Luke, the consummate story teller, is unlikely to have missed the opportunity to extract every last ounce of pathos from such a curious birth-place, instead of which he dismisses the apparent inconvenience in half a line.

If the wise men visit the new-born Jesus in Bethlehem, the traditional 6 January date is not beyond credibility, as Jesus would not have had to return to his family home in Nazareth to be circumcised; this, in turn, allows Jesus to be presented some forty days after his birth before Joseph receives a warning to flee into Egypt. At the end of Matthew's account the knotty Bethlehem/Nazareth problem is solved by Joseph fearing to return to his native city and opting to settle in Nazareth instead but, of course, this throws the Lucan tax registration scenario into doubt as, if Joseph lived in Bethlehem, he would not have had to travel there.

I have used material from Sura 19 of the Qu'ran in Act 2 Scene 2, and acknowledge its proper status as believed by hundreds of millions to be sacredly inspired Scripture; where it contradicts the New Testament, over the nature of the child, for example, I have taken a Christian standpoint.

In all other respects I have allowed the text, particularly from Luke, to speak for itself. In spite of quite proper doubts about the notion of a census of tax payers and the known dates of Quirinius's rule (Luke 2.1–2), I have let these and other similar events stand as this, except in respect of the two instances above, is largely a traditional play on the basis that it is theology and not consistency that is crucial, and that unnecessary disturbance would cause unnecessary distraction from my central purpose.

That is not to say that a traditional play must adopt the traditions of later ages. I do not accept, for example, that Jesus was born "In The Bleak Midwinter", as Christina Rosetti would have it, still experiencing the Little Ice Age whose conclusion some scholars date as late as 1870, and when the Victorians were adopting Germanic Midwinter Solstice customs.

As the purpose of the play is primarily theological, it would be impossible to follow the Jewish custom of not citing the name of God and so there are, if you like, theological anachronisms. Likewise, the Prologue delivered by God and the Epilogue delivered by the Holy Spirit paradoxically advance somewhat complex theological arguments by being somewhat anthropomorphic in the spirit of medieval mystery plays and, indeed, my mind, particularly in writing humorous passages, was never very far from them.

I should also say a word about the use of the term "Jeshua" for the Messiah, which caused some disquiet when I used it in my companion *Parish Passion Play*. This is not an attempt to be idiosyncratic for the sake of it; apart from the fact that Jeshua is what his contemporaries would have called him, the word provides more flexibility in writing blank verse than "Jesus".

The dates at the beginning of each scene are not supposed to be scientifically precise but indicate a credible chronology except, of course, when appearing at the head of the Prologue and Epilogue when they might pass as a mild joke. I follow the Jewish custom of calendar dating from sunset to sunset which explains the birth of Jesus on the 25th on the evening of the natural day when the sun rose on the 24th. I am aware of the scholarship which dates the birth of Jesus to 4 BC but this hardly works in a traditional play! It would make a very clumsy play if dates were somehow to be inserted into the dialogue so it will help audiences if they are included in the performance programme.

The play can either be read by participants sitting in a horseshoe and rising to read their lines as indicated, or it can be acted. The text is written so that a reading without actions makes sense and this accounts for the absence of stage directions; for example, when a shepherd touches the new-born child it can be assumed that he is either bending low or kneeling, according to the preference of the director; but he is certainly not standing up straight. The play is written in traditional blank verse because, in my experience, and perhaps counter-intuitively, this form forces the reader subconsciously to place emphasis on the words that require it whereas prose demands a great deal more rehearsal.

The characters of God, Jeshua and the Holy Spirit speak in three-line stanzas, or terces, which symbolise their mutual membership of the Trinity. This form of verse is not easy to deliver and, alone in the play, requires an experienced reader of poetry.

When the term "severally" is used in directions it means that the speakers should select some of the text offered and say it but not in unison.

My intention is that a performance should only require one rehearsal, largely to check the sound system, if one is being used, and to accustom readers to the tempo. The play consists of many very short scenes and there should be no gaps between them so that the momentum is maintained, reflecting the modern techniques of radio and television drama rather than a more ponderous theatrical tradition.

A straight performance will take 75 minutes but some directors may wish to include carols, and it would be a novelty to open the play, instead of closing it, with "We Three Kings".

Above all, the purpose of the play is to restore Christmas to its proper theological context. If we are simply to make do with Nativity plays for children with their tea-towel head-dresses and tinsel angel wings, they will be put aside like "childish things" (1 Corinthians 13.11) when we grow up, or at least grow older. We can, and should, do better.

Kevin Carey
Advent Sunday 2015

Parish Nativity Play

CONTENTS

Preface v
Dramatis Personae xiii
A Parish Nativity Play 1

PROLOGUE 2

ACT 1 5
SCENE 1:   The Library of Alexandria 5
SCENE 2:   The Temple Sanctuary, Jerusalem 8
SCENE 3:   The Temple Court of the Same 10
SCENE 4:   Zechariah's House, The Judean Hills 10
SCENE 5:   Joachim's House, Nazareth 11
SCENE 6:   Joseph's House, Nazareth 19
SCENE 7:   Joachim's House, Nazareth 21
SCENE 8:   Zechariah's House 23
SCENE 9:   Zechariah's House, The Judean Hills 25

ACT 2 29
SCENE 1:   The Library of Alexandria 29
SCENE 2:   A Road outside Bethlehem 30
SCENE 3:   Outside the Library of Alexandria 32
SCENE 4:   Bethlehem 33
SCENE 5:   The Egyptian Desert 35
SCENE 6:   Jacob's House 35
SCENE 7:   The Roof of Jacob's House 36
SCENE 8:   A Field outside Bethlehem 37
SCENE 9:   Jacob's House, Bethlehem 40
SCENE 10: The Roof of Jacob's House 42
SCENE 11: A Field outside Bethlehem 43

ACT 3	....	**45**
SCENE 1:	Jacob's House, Bethlehem	45
SCENE 2:	King Herod's Palace, Jerusalem	46
SCENE 3:	An Inn in Bethlehem	50
SCENE 4:	Jacob's House, Bethlehem	51
SCENE 5:	An Inn in Bethlehem	56
SCENE 6:	Another Inn, Bethlehem	56
SCENE 7:	The Temple in Jerusalem	57
SCENE 8:	King Herod's Palace, Jerusalem	60
SCENE 9:	An Inn, Jerusalem	61
SCENE 10:	The Temple Court, Jerusalem	62
EPILOGUE	....	**65**

DRAMATIS PERSONAE
In order of appearance

1. GOD
2. BALTHASAR—supposed King of Tarse and Egypt
3. MELCHIOR—supposed King of Arabia
4. CASPAR—supposed King of Sheba, Ethiopia and Yemen
5. ZECHARIAH—a priest
6. The Angel GABRIEL
7. ELIZABETH—wife to Zechariah and cousin of Mary
8. ANNA—Mother of Mary
9. MARY—Daughter of Joachim and Anna, Mother of Jeshua
10. JOACHIM—Mary's father
11. JOSEPH—Mary's betrothed
12. RABBI
13. GUEST 1
14. GUEST 2
15. JACOB—Joseph's cousin
16. ESTHER—Jacob's wife
17. SHEPHERD 1
18. SHEPHERD 2
19. SHEPHERD 3
20. King HEROD
21. A SERVANT
22. ADVISER 1 to King Herod
23. ADVISER 1 to King Herod
24. DIPLOMAT
25. An INN KEEPER
26. A STRANGER
27. ANNA—woman in the Temple

28. SIMEON
29. ELDER 1
30. ELDER 2
31. JESHUA
32. The HOLY SPIRIT

A PARISH NATIVITY PLAY

PROLOGUE: **Heaven**
23 September 1 BC
GOD

GOD: In love projected and in love fulfilled,
beautiful flesh made solid from thin air,
created in perfection as I willed,
set in a grove where man might dance and share
in earthly freedom something yet of me,
angelic calm and sweetness without care.
And yet, in my sublime naivety,
full of my generous self, as you might say,
or class it as a sacred heresy,
I failed to understand the human way,
that love depends on freedom to deny,
to sacrifice or follow its own way,
that only love from choice can satisfy
my need for human love bravely perfected.
Else why would I create? I know not why!

O sacred flaw which I in man injected
to satisfy this generous need in me,
from which for all time he must be protected.
As mine was lost, man lost naivety;
I saw it coming but could not prevent,
as Eve stood rapt before the knowledge tree,
the coiling argument of the serpent;
but was it he who spoke or was it me?
Whichever, it was too late to relent.

Parish Nativity Play PROLOGUE

Again, naive as only God can be
residing in the permanently sublime,
I soon regretted what I had set free
—not in an earthly sequence bound by time
but knowing all things simultaneously,
perceiving in an instant every crime—
my poor reward, a scant minority,
the greater number waxing proud and bold
thinking themselves creators more than me.

But now my world of love is shrunk and cold,
from Eden to today without a pause
my prophets snubbed, my tribute bought and sold,
my generous spirit narrowed to harsh laws,
my name used for oppression and advance,
where every act must have a moral cause,
where bad faith is assumed and circumstance
—whether the case is black, or white, or grey—
outweighs the role of motive and of chance.
Pride, discontent with innocence and play,
raising itself to dole out punishment
in my name led my wandering flock astray.
Robed wolves, disguised as shepherds, cruelly bent
my flock towards them, and away from me,
saying I would not listen nor relent.

PROLOGUE *Parish Nativity Play*

Law is a shadow of theology,
concerned with prosecution and defence,
indifferent to the flaw of being free;
and so my abstract stance of immanence
gave far too full a rein to piety
at the expense of feeling and of sense,
leaving too great a stress on liberty,
leading to speculation and distress
as heart and mind were caught in enmity
instead of simple love and quietness,
the head too dominant, the heart repressed,
the two reversed in volatility.

But now I am resolved to bring man rest
by transparently making my amends
to those whom my benevolence has repressed,
that God and man may re-unite as friends,
the priestly hierarchy swept away,
a final covenant until life ends,
in which my lambs might safely go astray.
I will in my own self become my son
walking with man his steep and crooked way,
finishing lovingly what was begun.
My Chosen People will at last proclaim,
by witnessing what I have said and done,
my goodness to the world in Jesus' name.
Your players, simple, shunning all disguises,
will tell my story in a brand new frame
for your delight. Prepare for some surprises!

ACT 1

SCENE 1: **The Library of Alexandria**
23 September 1 BC
BALTHASAR, MELCHIOR, CASPAR

BALTHASAR: Well met, good friends, in Alexandria. Melchior and Caspar, you are welcome here.

MELCHIOR: We thank you for your welcome, Balthasar. This library is even more splendid than the accounts of travellers I have heard. Look at the wealth of manuscripts, Caspar!

CASPAR: I have not seen the like of this before. Balthasar, we could spend our whole lives here and still not read all that you have to show.

BALTHASAR: True, gentlemen. But shall we now proceed? A strange conjunction forecast for the heavens has strangely brought you to this learned place. Melchior, being the eldest, please speak first.

MELCHIOR: For more than twenty years I have been bent on gleaning earthly fortunes from the stars; and recently, only a year ago, I thought I saw a unique conjunction which prompted me to leave Arabia and travel here to verify my view.

ACT 1, SCENE 1   *Parish Nativity Play*

BALTHASAR: Caspar, you are the youngest of us here, famed among scholars for adventurous thoughts; do you accord with learned Melchior?

CASPAR: The heavens may portend a strange conjunction, as Melchior has calculated, but my forecast is more radical than his: a comet, even brighter than the moon, will soon rise from the eastern horizon and hover over Judea for twelve days.

BALTHASAR: How long from now will this event occur?

CASPAR: Precisely sixteen solar months from now.

BALTHASAR: Your calculation accords with my view based on my reading of the Jewish texts. For centuries their prophets have foretold a saviour, or Messiah, for their race, descended from David, their priest and king, and consequently, this saviour will be born in the home of David, Bethlehem. I therefore stake my reputation on this comet shining on Bethlehem.

MELCHIOR: I am too old to change my settled ways, to conflate passion with astrology, but youth must have its say and have its day.

BALTHASAR: Bravely and humbly spoken, Melchior. Let me outline to you our future plan: we will resume our studies separately and, if our views are unchanged in a year, we will reconvene here to set our course to see the comet over Bethlehem.

MELCHIOR: If age permits I will come back again.

CASPAR: What Balthasar has said is critical; although it will be splendid in itself, the comet is a sign of great events.

BALTHASAR: Well, gentlemen, fifteen months from today, if all goes well, we will all meet and then observe the comet over Bethlehem.

SCENE 2: **The Temple Sanctuary, Jerusalem**
24 September 1 BC
ZECHARIAH, GABRIEL

ZECHARIAH: Prayers before incense have been offered up. The greatest honour of my priestly life has come at last. I never thought it would. Some priests serve their whole lives within these walls without being drawn by lot to offer incense. Once Abijah's term is over I will leave, retire, and sit beneath my well loved trees, my duty done. How sweet the incense smells!
(PAUSE)
A taper, and the smoke will soon ascend to cheer the people watching from the Court. Lower the flame.

GABRIEL: (STAND)

ZECHARIAH: What's that, I say, what's that? My eyes are almost blinded! To my right the Temple is ablaze. I must retire.

GABRIEL: Fear not, good Zechariah, pray, fear not!

ZECHARIAH: How can I see you and not be afraid? I never saw the like; what does this mean?

GABRIEL: Fear not, I say, the Lord has heard your prayer, though uttered humbly your wish is clear. By God's command, Elizabeth, your wife, will bear a son as servant to the Lord, named John by you when he is circumcised. His birth will bring great joy throughout the land, not just to you but to all who accept that he is great in the sight of the Lord; even before his birth he will be filled with the Holy Spirit; but he must forego, in recognition of his vocation, wine and strong drink. And he will surely turn many of Israel's people back to God. In the spirit and power of Elijah parental hearts will turn to their children, the disobedient back to righteousness, to make his people ready for their Lord.

ZECHARIAH: How will I know that this may come about? My wife and I are far too old for this.

GABRIEL: I am the angel Gabriel. I stand within God's presence and I have been sent to speak to you and bring you this good news; but now, because you have doubted my news, which will be fulfilled in God's own good time, you will be mute, incapable of speech, until these things have come to pass. Farewell. God's servants will fulfil what I foretell.

SCENE 3: **The Temple Court of the Same**
24 September 1 BC
CROWD

CROWD: (SEVERALLY)
Here he comes now; he has been such a time. Look, he is signing to us, he is mute. He is struck dumb! He cannot say a word! He must have seen a vision from the Lord!

SCENE 4: **Zechariah's House, The Judean Hills**
25 October 1 BC
ELIZABETH, ZECHARIAH (MUTE)

ELIZABETH: Home early, husband! What a nice surprise! But you look strangely vacant, what is wrong? Stop looking at me like that! Say something! There is no point asking me to calm down! It only makes me worse. What has gone wrong? A writing tablet? Are you really mute?
(PAUSE)
An angel of the Lord named Gabriel promised from God that we shall have a son! I should not say 'What nonsense!' but I must. To think that you and I at our great age should be expected

to resort to that! Shame on you if you think you have the strength to re-enact our youth so late in life. If God wills what the angel says He wills there must be nicer ways than doing that! (PAUSE)

Manoah, you write, and his barren wife who, prompted by an angel, bore Samson; much good it did if I remember right. Well, if God wills, we hardly have a choice if you are to regain your muted voice.

SCENE 5: **Joachim's House, Nazareth**
25 March 1 AD
ANNA, MARY, JOACHIM, GABRIEL, JOSEPH

ANNA: Although a girl must attend to her prayers, it is more proper for the men to pray. Now Mary, come quickly, you have your chores!

MARY: Mother, I recognise the truth you say but I am strangely called to watch and pray: I cannot help but think of your namesake Hannah, who bore the holy Samuel proclaiming him the hope of Israel; of Samson's mother and other women who dedicated themselves to the Lord. I would not claim to be equal with them in trying to imitate their holy lives, modelling myself on their selflessness.

ACT 1, SCENE 5 — *Parish Nativity Play*

ANNA: Nonsense, girl! Those heroic times are past when our forebears bore witness to the Lord. As subjects of King Herod and of Rome our self-respect has gone, our piety reduced to observation of the law. Still, even though your prayers are rather long, I should not scold you. As your father says, a girl can find many worse activities than praying. I will leave you for a while to see what I can find at the market. We can complete our chores when I return.
(SITS)

MARY: Oh dear! I want to please mother and God; I wish they were agreed what I should do; still, I must bear my mother's discontent with quiet patience and humility.

JOACHIM: (STANDS)
Why, Mary, praying still? Well, never mind, I will not scold you as your mother does; I want to see the best in both of you, not taking sides because she disagrees with your too time-consuming piety. I will leave you; you need the peace until your mother comes back from the market-place.
(SITS)

MARY:	Oh dear! I do not want to place my father in a position where he thinks he must choose between me and mother. (PAUSE) Let me pray, for if we have the discord without prayer it will have gone for nothing. Let me pray.
GABRIEL:	(STANDS) Hail Mary, highly favoured of the Lord! Do not be frightened, for I bring good news. You will conceive today and bear a son whom you will call Jeshua, the holy one. He will be great, the Son of the most high, and God his Father will give him the throne of David, your great ancestor; he will rule the house of Jacob forever, and of his kingdom there will be no end.
MARY:	Good news it may be but I am perplexed! How can this be as I am but a maid?
GABRIEL:	The Holy Spirit will settle on you, therefore the potency of the Most High will overshadow you with vital grace; the child born to you will be holy, and he is and will be called the Son of God.
MARY:	How can such grace and favour come to me? How shall I deal with its enormity?

ACT 1, SCENE 5   *Parish Nativity Play*

GABRIEL: Mary, my good news is not finished yet! Your cousin, the devout Elizabeth, dismissed as too old to conceive a child, is six months pregnant with a son from God; you see, all things are possible with him.

MARY: Look down on me, the servant of the Lord; let all be done according to His word.

GABRIEL: Your answer, given in humility, will set in motion what will prove to be the greatest act in human history. Farewell! Remember, do not be afraid! The Lord is with you, mother yet a maid! (SITS)

MARY: I am amazed! Then let me try to pray to calm myself. Prayer is so difficult, often disturbed by trivial events, then how can I be calm now I have heard what God intends for me, and I for him? There are such mighty issues to resolve. (PAUSE)
God in heaven, whose angel I have seen, (PAUSE)
How will I tell Joseph and my parents? How will I broach the subject of the child? My sacred trust is close to my disgrace, and they will see the trouble in my face. Yet I must calm myself or I am lost.
(PAUSE)

JOSEPH: (STANDS)

Parish Nativity Play   ACT 1, SCENE 5

MARY: Joseph! You here when I am quite alone.

JOSEPH: I know the custom, yet you are too stern. For more than six months we have been betrothed, firm in our love yet counting on reserve, yours as a maid, mine as a mature man. Your face is flushed; your eyes are strangely bright. Are you unwell? What can I do to help?

MARY: My state is far stranger than love's sickness: I am in love with God, and God with me.

JOSEPH: When human love is part of loving God why would we want to separate the two? In what you say, I hope you still love me?

MARY: I love you more now than I ever loved when first your father brought you to our home, but our love must be subject to God's will and I—we—must bear a sacred charge. Joseph, sit down, listen, but do not look. While I am speaking, face the other way. (PAUSE) An angel has delivered God's request that I should bear a sacred child for him to be the saviour of the Jewish race. The Spirit of the Lord will soon descend, transforming my poor flesh that it may bear the Messiah, to be called Jeshua. I have consented to this awesome task and you must help me to keep to my word. Now you may look at me to see the truth.

ACT 1, SCENE 5 *Parish Nativity Play*

JOSEPH: You are so pious and so sensible it would be difficult to doubt your word, yet what you ask is far too much for me to take in without further thought and prayer. What has been asked, to which you have agreed, will certainly be seen as your disgrace. When you have talked to your father and mother I will return tomorrow to decide how you can be protected from yourself. (SITS)

MARY: Lord, I know you will keep your word to me! Protect me from insult and infamy!

JOACHIM: (STANDS)
I have just seen Joseph hurrying away; head bowed, he would not look me in the eye. Is he ashamed of being here with you? I know the rules are strict in such a case. Your mother is a stickler for form but you both know that I am always fair. Has something happened to disrupt your love? Have you quarrelled? I pray it is not so.

MARY: Father, my dear, we have not disagreed. I had something so difficult to say to Joseph, no less difficult for you. I am to bear a child ordained by God. An angel brought his message and I vowed to do his will as his humble servant.

Parish Nativity Play   ACT 1, SCENE 5

JOACHIM: Your prayers have carried you beyond belief. What news is this? Young girls have sometimes strayed but never have I heard of such a way of justifying what we know is wrong.

MARY: As I will do as God has asked of me, God will ensure that I am justified.

JOACHIM: And what does Joseph say as your betrothed?

MARY: He will return when we have found accord.

JOACHIM: I could not expect less from such a man; Joseph is steady and will not be rash. Your mother, though, is quite another thing.

MARY: Our hope is truth; there is no other way. My mother will be angry for a while. We must have faith that what the angel said will be made clear to Joseph and to you.

ANNA: (STANDS)
The prices are impossibly high! They seem to go up every single day! Why are you both looking at me like that? What has happened while I have been away?

MARY: Mother, please listen to what I must say. Do not break in. Please hear me to the end.

ANNA: A strange request for one as young as you. I expect you know what she has to say.

ACT 1, SCENE 5   *Parish Nativity Play*

JOACHIM: She must speak for herself. Now, let her speak.

MARY: An angel of the Lord has come to me, asking that I should bear the Messiah, conceived by God's power through the Holy Spirit. I have consented and have told Joseph. Please wait; I have a final piece of news. The angel said Elizabeth is with child, for six months now bearing a holy son. I want to go to her but I must wait until Joseph and you have understood God's will for me. He will come here tomorrow.

ANNA: Am I going mad? The world is upside-down!

JOACHIM: At least Joseph is calm. Let us all pray and say nothing we might come to regret. The situation is fraught enough without rash statements. Joseph must decide to reject Mary or make her his bride. If he rejects her, then she might be best lodged with Elizabeth until her child is born and we can find a plausible story to minimise our family shame. If this is God's will, he must send us aid to protect Mary, pregnant yet a maid.

SCENE 6: **Joseph's House, Nazareth**
25 March 1 AD
JOSEPH, GABRIEL

JOSEPH: I never could have dreamed of such a thing of Mary whom I have known since a child! To disbelieve her is impossible since I have never known her tell a lie, nor known her do a bad deed, come to that! Yet I must face the situation with which we are confronted rationally. How she can know that she is now with child is difficult enough knowing that it was conceived today; it then follows that it cannot be an ordinary child given life in the ordinary way. Her virtue is intact beyond a doubt, but that is not the issue we must face. By the Holy Spirit, with child or not—and I accept her word, reluctantly—I must protect my darling from herself until the child is born; then we will see what kind of child it is that comes of this. If things turn out the way the angel says, with Mary bringing forth the Messiah, I must be shrewd, following a middle course, protecting Mary and heeding God's word.

GABRIEL: (STANDS)
Be not afraid, Joseph, Son of David! Peace be with you; my name is Gabriel, the same angel that came to your betrothed bringing good news for Jews and all mankind. Her consent to bear God's son, Jeshua, the Spirit's child, has caused great joy in heaven. Let me repeat, just for your peace of mind, Mary, your wife-to-be, will bear a son named Jeshua, sent from on high to save his people. Do you follow what I say?

JOSEPH: Yes, I believe! Yet your news is as hard to take as it was when I heard it first! The repetition does not ease surprise! Pardon my shrewdness, it was kindly meant.

GABRIEL: Your shrewdness does you credit. Take Mary to be your wife as soon as possible. That is the best protection you can give to her unsullied reputation. People will wonder at the sudden haste but that amounts to much less than her shame. Peace be with you. The Lord will be with you.
(SITS)

JOSEPH: Was that an angel or was it a dream? It does not matter much; my course is clear. Now I recall something Isaiah says: "A virgin shall conceive and bear a son who shall be called Emmanuel, God with us." I wonder whether what the prophet says refers to Mary. That would make good sense. Before I sleep, let me give thanks and pray in preparation for our wedding day.

SCENE 7: **Joachim's House, Nazareth**
26 March 1 AD
JOACHIM, JOSEPH, ANNA, RABBI, MARY

JOACHIM: The sun is hardly up and Joseph here! I did not think to see him here so soon.

JOSEPH: (STANDS) Blessings upon this house! I bring good news. The same angel that appeared to Mary appeared to me last night and said the same words that he had said to her of the child. But, as our neighbours will not understand, to protect Mary from unjust scandal, we must be married at once, immediately! In this way Mary's holy pregnancy will appear natural. See, I have brought the Rabbi so that we may act at once.

JOACHIM: Since your respected father gave consent to your betrothal to my lovely girl it has been difficult to challenge you. You always have an answer that is just.

ACT 1, SCENE 7   *Parish Nativity Play*

ANNA: This talk of angels makes me frightened but you men seem to have come to an accord. What do you say, Rabbi? What should we do?

RABBI: The talk of angels is unusual but Mary's situation is acute. You have been betrothed for more than six months; you know your minds and will not deviate. A wedding is a communal affair which does not mean there needs to be a feast. Let us fix on tomorrow at sunset. A later day will do to celebrate.

MARY: And then I will be free to go away to visit my cousin, Elizabeth, and stay with her until her child is born.

JOSEPH: Your absence will relieve me of much pain as we must not behave as man and wife until you are delivered of the child.

MARY: I knew the Lord would take care of our needs; he has fulfilled his promise with good deeds.

SCENE 8: **Zechariah's House**
5 April 1 AD
ELIZABETH, MARY, ZECHARIAH (MUTE)

ELIZABETH: To think that at my age I should conceive, hiding from friends to avoid ridicule, with Zechariah not much company although his hands are always comforting. But what I want is his outpoured advice, not scanty words scratched on his writing tablet! My coyness must come shortly to an end as I will want for women's company as the time draws nearer to my full term. Who's that walking so fast? I know her step; just when I talked of women's company.

MARY: (STANDS)
I heard of your good news from Gabriel, the same that spoke God's word to Zechariah; we are both blessed. How strange that it is so.

ELIZABETH: I cannot stand! The child within me leaps with lively greeting for your presence here, stirred by the Holy Spirit to rejoice! Among the world's women, blessed are you, and blessed is the young fruit of your womb! Why, then, has this great blessing come to me, that the mother of God should visit me? And blessed she who believed there would be fulfilment of what she heard from the Lord.

ACT 1, SCENE 8 — *Parish Nativity Play*

MARY: With new-born grace, I magnify the Lord, and my soul rejoices in my God and Saviour, for he has looked upon me favourably, his poor handmaiden, lowly as I am, and for his sake all time will call me blessed. The mighty God has done great things for me and holy is his name above all names. His mercy is on all those who fear him from the beginning to the end of time. He has shown strength with his almighty arm, scattering the proud in their deluded hearts; he has put down the mighty from their thrones and lifted up the lowly and the meek; he has filled all the hungry with good things and empty-handed sent the rich away. Remembering his mercy, he has helped his servant Israel by honouring the promise he made to our ancestors, to Abraham and to his seed forever.

ELIZABETH: Praise be to God. Good Hannah's prayer made new!

MARY: Our children will be heirs to Samuel.

ELIZABETH: But yours will be immeasurably above my son John, although he will lead the way.

MARY: Until his circumcision I will stay.

ELIZABETH: How can my house be worthy of your womb?

MARY: Whether the difference is large or small we both serve God in answer to his call.

SCENE 9: **Zechariah's House, The Judean Hills**
3 July 1 AD
ELIZABETH, MARY, ZECHARIAH (INITIALLY MUTE), RABBI, GUEST 1, GUEST 2

ELIZABETH: Now everything is settled but the name; in spite of what the angel has laid down, my in-laws will not rest without a change back to our time-honoured Levitic names.

MARY: Have faith, Elizabeth, all will be well. Look how the birth was smooth, though you are old.

ELIZABETH: Of course you are right, Mary, when you say that, as God is with us, all will be well in spite of what we feel and others say.

MARY: I did not mean to scold with piety.

ELIZABETH: There, there! To be old is not to be wise.

ZECHARIAH: (STANDS)

ACT 1, SCENE 9 — *Parish Nativity Play*

ELIZABETH: At least today should be the final time we have to use this wretched writing tablet.
(PAUSE)
His name is John. Yes. That is nothing new. We have not changed our minds since the first day the angel told him what his name would be. When you get your voice back you will be right to scold the family for its dissent.

RABBI: (STANDS)

ELIZABETH: But now is not the time. Welcome Rabbi!

RABBI: During surgery I will say the name.

ELIZABETH: His name is John. No other name will do.

GUEST 1: But no-one in our family is called John. Like his father, he should be Zechariah!

GUEST 2: The name is nothing short of scandalous. It is not right to call a Levite John.

ELIZABETH: It is useless waving your arms like that. See, "John" is written in my husband's hand!

RABBI: Admittedly it is unusual but we seem to live in unusual times. John's mission under God will be revealed when he grows up. The name will then make sense.
(PAUSE)
I name you John just as your father writes. Now wrap him carefully; my job is done.

ZECHARIAH: Forgive me, Lord, for my perversity; I have paid dearly for it, rightfully. But now that I have seen all come to pass that the angel related faithfully, my heart is bursting to proclaim your Word:
Blessed be the Lord God of Israel
who has visited and redeemed his people;
and has raised up for us a mighty one,
a saviour from the house of his servant King David,
as his prophets long foretold,
that we might be saved from our enemies,
from hands that would destroy his chosen ones.
Thus he has shown the mercy he proclaimed
to our forebears, and faithfully renewed
his holy covenant with Abraham
that, rescued from the clutches of our foes,
we might worship him, innocent of fear,
in holiness all the days of our life.
And you, my son, prophet of the Most High,
will go before the Lord as his herald,
in order that his way should be prepared
to make salvation known to his people
through the forgiveness of their many sins.
And, by the tender mercy of our God,
the dayspring from on high will burst on us,
lightening those who languish in the dark
and in the shadow of impending death,
to guide our feet into the way of peace.

ACT 1, SCENE 9   *Parish Nativity Play*

GUEST 1:   I never heard such a strange thing before; it will be the talk of the neighbourhood.

GUEST 2:   How are we to make sense of what he said? Is he a prophet or a charlatan?

ELIZABETH: Shame! You have heard my husband prophesy. His age and situation must allow no doubt but proper weight to what he says. The child is named, time for ill feeling passed: let us unite before this holy child.

GUEST 1:   And Mary pregnant: what a family!

GUEST 2:   An outward show of holiness conceals a deal of wrong behind a tranquil face.

MARY: Elizabeth, ignore those cruel words! Pride is indifferent to argument. Farewell, cousin, I must be on my way to make ready for my momentous day.

ACT 2

SCENE 1: **The Library of Alexandria**
23 December 1 AD
BALTHASAR, MELCHIOR, CASPAR

BALTHASAR: Brothers, welcome! In your view does the sky portend what it promised a year ago? Melchior, pray speak first as is your right.

MELCHIOR: Nothing has changed to mar my reckoning; the conjunction I forecast is assured. Now let me add a vital element: the studies I have made assure me that what I have forecast will be marvellous; the skies portend a new age for mankind, a change of fortune for our suffering world.

BALTHASAR: Melchior, spoken well, we both agree. My studies, too, have taken such a turn; I am convinced that what we both foresee is the birth of the Jewish Messiah, of benefit to all, not just the Jews for, as their prophet Isaiah has said, their saviour will reach outward to the world. But Caspar, please speak now. I did not mean to leave you out; tell us what you have learned.

ACT 2, SCENE 2 — *Parish Nativity Play*

CASPAR: Although comets are notoriously hard to track as their appearance is so rare, I am convinced the new light in the East will grow yet brighter and come still nearer in its auspicious visit to our earth. In spite of my certainty I should say its trajectory is anomalous.

BALTHASAR: Or maybe we should say miraculous, if God most high is party in the case. The planetary conjunction augurs well. Now we have summarised all that we know, let us prepare; tomorrow we will go. I think, good gentlemen, we are agreed, to follow wherever the light might lead.

SCENE 2: A Road outside Bethlehem
24 December 1 AD
MARY, JOSEPH

MARY: My labour has begun, I am in pain; please, Joseph, let us stop here for a while.

JOSEPH: We must balance your need for rest, Mary, against the need to find a proper place where you can bear the child as he deserves.

MARY: From what the women said, it will be hours before the child is born; God will provide.

Parish Nativity Play   ACT 2, SCENE 2

JOSEPH:	We suffer from an oppressive edict! The registration is arbitrary. I guess Quirinius was given no choice; Emperor Augustus cannot be denied. No power on earth can contradict his word. (PAUSE) But look! A miracle from out of air, a date palm in full fruit this time of year and, right before our eyes as we stand here, a stream of water has begun to flow. Refresh yourself and eat; it is God's will.
MARY:	Such cool, clear water. I will wash my face but my condition makes me disinclined to eat although the dates are very fine.
JOSEPH:	But this is sacred food to give you strength.
MARY:	How right you are to prompt me to obey, for this is God's provision, as you say. (PAUSE) Such sweetness. Now my pain has gone away.
JOSEPH:	Although the sun is almost overhead we will achieve our journey's end today.
MARY:	Let us continue, then, without delay! More than I have received I could not ask to give me strength for my forthcoming task.

SCENE 3: **Outside the Library of Alexandria**
24 December 1 AD
BALTHASAR, MELCHIOR, CASPAR

BALTHASAR: Although I would prefer to travel straight to Bethlehem, courtesy demands that we should tell King Herod what we plan; it is his territory, after all, in name at least, as Caesar's puppet king.

MELCHIOR: And it would be most interesting to learn what his advisers say about our quest.

CASPAR: But surely we know all we need to know. The heavenly body rising in the East seems to have stopped not very far from here, above Bethlehem by my reckoning. If Herod does not like what we propose he might detain us for his selfish ends.

MELCHIOR: Herod is wily, I will give you that, but there is no avoiding what you say, Balthasar. We must do what you think right.

CASPAR: What will we find when we reach Bethlehem?

BALTHASAR: As I have said before, the ancient texts revered by the Jews promise a child sent from God to redeem his captive race. This Messiah, as he is called, will reign over his people as a priest and king.

CASPAR: Will he wage war? Will he overthrow Rome?

BALTHASAR: Be careful what you ask! You never know who might be listening to what we say. Dictators cannot flourish without spies!

MELCHIOR: The Greeks have numerous exotic myths which tell how gods and men are intertwined.

BALTHASAR: Unless he is to be an Alexander, I doubt the omens portend a soldier. As for the traffic between gods and men, the Jews are far too serious to accept the exotic, let alone the immoral! The sun has passed its zenith. Let us go, to take advantage of the gentler light; we have four hours before the fall of night.

SCENE 4: **Bethlehem**
25 December 1 AD
JOSEPH, MARY, JACOB, ESTHER

JOSEPH: A few steps more; the house is now in sight.

MARY: Thank God! I am exhausted, and the child will soon be born. God's promise will be kept. I know I never would be asked to bear hardship beyond my means. God is with me.

JOSEPH: Now, here is cousin Jacob's house at last. Hello! Your cousin Joseph comes in need!

ACT 2, SCENE 4   *Parish Nativity Play*

JACOB: (STANDS) What did you say? Who knocks so late at night? What do you want? My family are asleep!

JOSEPH: Your cousin Joseph, as I have just said, and my wife Mary, about to give birth!

JACOB: Your wife, indeed! Just let me find my robe. Here are the keys. I will unlock the door.

JOSEPH: I fear there is no time for courtesies; Mary is on the verge of giving birth!

JACOB: A new wife and a baby born so soon!

JOSEPH: There will be time for quibbles, but not now. Her labour is far gone. Please call your wife.

JACOB: Esther, come quickly! You are wanted here.

ESTHER: (STANDS)

JACOB: This is our cousin Joseph and his wife; he says she is about to have a child.

ESTHER: "He says! He says!" You men! Just look at her!

JACOB: But they are barely married...

ESTHER: Never mind. Come in! Stop chattering and shut the door! Mary's urgent needs must be satisfied; then we can argue about family pride.

SCENE 5: **The Egyptian Desert**
25 December 1 AD
CASPAR

CASPAR: How bright the night sky is with that strange light! Yes, it has stopped its movement for two nights. The time is now; I feel the throb of life, new energy injected in the earth, divine involvement in man's history, engendered by a long-expected birth. I pray we will arrive in time to see the due fulfilment of this mystery.

SCENE 6: **Jacob's House**
25 December 1 AD
ESTHER, JACOB, JOSEPH, MARY

ESTHER: The house is full to bursting with our kin; all come to register at Caesar's call!

JACOB: A curse upon him and his precious tax!

ESTHER: You men, make yourselves scarce until I call.

JACOB, JOSEPH:
    (SIT)

ACT 2, SCENE 7 — *Parish Nativity Play*

ESTHER: The place for animals is swept and clean with new sand on the floor and sweet fresh hay in the manger where the child can be laid. Miriam, be quick, bring hot water and towels! The girl's contractions have become quite short! We must do everything within our power. The baby will be born within the hour.

SCENE 7: **The Roof of Jacob's House**
25 December 1 AD
JACOB, JOSEPH, ESTHER (OFF)

JACOB: Esther is a good woman; all the same I like to climb up here out of her way.

JOSEPH: I like it on the roof. Look at that star, or whatever it is. How bright it shines.

JACOB: There is no use in changing the subject. Joseph, what kind of trouble are you in? She's sweet enough, your girl, and quite pretty, but then you turn up here with a baby!

JOSEPH: Jacob, give me a moment, I am tired and anxious about Mary and the child. You see that star presaging something great? Mary says it shines to announce the birth, a special gift from God to all mankind.

JACOB: I have heard explanations in my time but none as strange as this; and you so shrewd.

JOSEPH:	Since Mary conceived by the power of God I have been forced to answer many times, which has helped me to reach a settled view: either you believe or you disbelieve. There are no words of mine that I can say to prove that Mary's child is divine.
ESTHER:	(STANDS) A boy! A boy! Mother and child are well! Come down at once now that the place is fit for men. The boy will be called Jeshua, born for us in the blazing of a star!

SCENE 8: **A Field outside Bethlehem**
25 December 1 AD
SHEPHERD 1, SHEPHERD 2, SHEPHERD 3, GABRIEL, ALL

SHEPHERD 1:	It's almost midnight but the sky's so bright I can't sleep; just look at that blazing star!
SHEPHERD 2:	It's quite amazing; something's going wrong. At least the sheep are quiet; that's good news.
SHEPHERD 3:	I've watched sheep in these hills for fifty years but never seen the like of this before.
SHEPHERD 2:	No good will come of it. It never does.
SHEPHERD 3:	Over the years our fortunes even out; there's no point worrying from day to day.

ACT 2, SCENE 8   *Parish Nativity Play*

SHEPHERD 2: It's all right for you now you're getting old but I have sons who need to find some work and daughters who need husbands before long. If that star is an omen of bad times it's poor people like us who will be hurt.

SHEPHERD 1: There's always work for boys in Sephoris; and pretty girls are never short of boys.

SHEPHERD 3: I went to Sephoris once. I hated it.

SHEPHERD 1: Well, never mind. We need to get some sleep (PAUSE)

GABRIEL: (STANDS)

SHEPHERD 1: Good God! What's that? It must be a bad dream! A blazing giant towering over me! I can't escape! I'm frozen to the spot!

GABRIEL: Fear not, good man, for yourself or the sheep! You are not dreaming. See, this glorious light comes from the Lord, as I! Peace be with you!

SHEPHERD 2: I knew that star would bring us something strange.

SHEPHERD 3: Be quiet and listen to what the vision says!

GABRIEL: I am the angel Gabriel, sent from God to bring good news, great joy for all mankind! Today is born to you in Bethlehem a saviour, the Messiah, Christ the Lord! And this is how to find the blessed child; he will be wrapped in winding bands of cloth and lying in an animals' feeding trough.

ALL OTHERS: (STAND; IN UNISON)
Glory to God in heaven; and peace on earth, for all will find great gladness from this birth.
(SIT)

SHEPHERD 1: All normal now except that blazing star! The angel by his words surely implied that we should find the child in Bethlehem.

SHEPHERD 2: I always knew that star would bring good luck.

SHEPHERD 1: We need to hurry! What about the sheep?

SHEPHERD 3: There's nothing that I haven't seen before. I don't mind staying if you want to go. Just carry my good wishes to the child and take a lamb for him. We can pretend it died on this damp night. They often do!

SHEPHERD 1: Thank you for being so gracious. Let us go to see if what the angel said is true.

SHEPHERD 2: To doubt an angel will bring us bad luck!

ACT 2, SCENE 9 *Parish Nativity Play*

SHEPHERD 1: I'm sorry; but let's go without delay not stopping for a minute on the way.

SCENE 9: **Jacob's House, Bethlehem**
25 December 1 AD
ESTHER, MARY, JOSEPH, JACOB, SHEPHERD 1, SHEPHERD 2

ESTHER: The baby is asleep. The Lord be praised!

MARY: And such an easy birth! Blessed be God!

JOSEPH: Now Mary, you must take much needed rest.

MARY: I promise, once the baby has been fed.

JOSEPH: Unlike most babies, Jeshua looks wise!

MARY: A sense of grandeur in those big, dark eyes!

ESTHER: He looks as if he's special. I admit.

JACOB: I feel it too, Joseph; I now believe your story of the baby's provenance.
(PAUSE)
What's that outside? It's late for such a noise. By now the drunks have usually gone home. I'll chase them so as not to wake the child. You there, playing that pipe. Just cut it out! Don't push past me and violate my house!

SHEPHERD 1, SHEPHERD 2:
(STAND)

SHEPHERD 1: We're celebrating! Is this the right place? Why look, it's just like what the angel said! A baby wrapped in winding bands of cloth sleeping within the animals' feeding trough!

JACOB: Angel! Whatever next? What's that you say?

SHEPHERD 1: Calm down, my friend, no need to be annoyed.

JACOB: Telling me to calm down makes me more tense. And I am not your friend. Just tell your tale.

SHEPHERD 1: An angel of the Lord appeared to us bringing good news and speaking of the child, explaining how we'd find him here tonight. Then there were angels shouting in a throng. And we have come just as the first one said.

MARY: Jacob, there is no reason for alarm. See, what they have said is all of a piece with everything connected with the child. Now, if you know a little lullaby play softly; it will please my wondrous child!

SHEPHERD 2: Our gaffer who's stayed behind with the sheep has sent a present of a little lamb; perhaps it will amuse your baby boy. May I bend down and lay it by the child?

MARY: There is nothing more lovely than a lamb. Ah! See him smile. A lamb and lullaby!

ESTHER:	Now let us leave mother and child in peace. Good shepherds, stay and take a little wine as first outside the family to see the child who, as you say, will bring good news.
SHEPHERD 1:	How strange it should be humble folk like us entrusted with the message from on high; we have few words to say what we have seen, but trust they will be equal to our task. Goodwill to mankind; good news for the poor! None will have heard the like of it before.

SCENE 10: **The Roof of Jacob's House**
25 December 1 AD
JACOB, JOSEPH

JACOB:	Before we go to sleep, just one more word. If this boy is all that the angel said, if he is the Messiah from the Lord, how will you make it known? What will you do to proclaim him the leader of us all? What will the temple leaders have to say? And what of Herod and the might of Rome?
JOSEPH:	The boy is hardly born. There will be time to think of how we must proceed with this, but we must take our guidance from on high; God will not let us down, depend on that. Look at the East; the dawn is on its way, a new dawn for us all this blessed day.

SCENE 11: **A Field outside Bethlehem**
25 December 1 AD

SHEPHERD 1, SHEPHERD 2, SHEPHERD 3

SHEPHERD 1: It happened as the angel said it would.

SHEPHERD 2: We gave the lamb to him on your behalf.

SHEPHERD 3: So wonderful. I've never heard the like. The sun is almost up. I will stay here but you must go and tell what you have seen. Tell the good news to all with all your might, then come back here before the fall of night.

ACT 2, SCENE 11   *Parish Nativity Play*

ACT 3

SCENE 1: **Jacob's House, Bethlehem**
1 January 2 AD
JOSEPH, JACOB, MARY

JOSEPH: Now that the boy-child has been circumcised we should return at once to Nazareth.

JACOB: If you go now you will hardly arrive before you have to set out once again to present Jeshua in the Temple. Now that most of our guests have registered to pay the Roman tax they will go home, leaving us room to entertain you here.

JOSEPH: You are so kind; my wife will be relieved. Here she comes now to thank you for herself.

MARY: (STANDS)

JOSEPH: Mary, it is precisely as you said, Jacob has kindly asked us to remain until we go up to Jerusalem to offer our first son, Jeshua, to God.

MARY: You are so kind. I feel that we must stay until God's light of glory goes away.

SCENE 2: **King Herod's Palace, Jerusalem**
4 January 2 AD
HEROD, BALTHASAR, MELCHIOR, CASPAR, SERVANT, ADVISER 1, ADVISER 2, DIPLOMAT

HEROD: Gentlemen, welcome, it is such a treat to host such scholars in Jerusalem, a pleasant change from ranting Temple priests who meddle in my marital affairs although I adhere to our Jewish Law. It is so dull here after life in Greece.

BALTHASAR: Where no doubt you studied philosophy.

HEROD: Ah yes, Balthasar, grave philosophy. The women were so gorgeous …

MELCHIOR: … and at Rome I daresay you studied military affairs.

HEROD: Of course, Melchior, affairs of many kinds! In military affairs the Roman way is nowadays to engage barbarians to fight their wars, so they are growing soft, on top of which they have no subtlety. Well, not the men, but you should see the girls!

CASPAR: They say their public buildings are immense.

HEROD: Not bad, Caspar, for western locations, but not a patch on Alexandria.

SERVANT: (STANDS)
The red wine you ordered, Your Majesty.

HEROD: Ah good, your welcome refreshments are here. As you drink you can say why you have come to visit me in dull Jerusalem. I doubt you came here for my company!

SERVANT: (SITS)

BALTHASAR: Our quest will not be a surprise to you. We seek the child who has, as you must know, but recently been born King of the Jews. We forecast, and then saw collectively, his heavenly sign arising in the East. If we are right, and we believe we are, this king we speak of is the Messiah. If this child were an ordinary prince we would not be here now consulting you. Once we have heard what your advisers say our purpose is to venerate the child.

HEROD: Of course! Of course! You were right to come here. You, servant dog—come here immediately!

SERVANT: (STANDS)

HEROD: Now, make yourselves at home; immediately! Show them their rooms! We will meet at dinner.

BALTHASAR, MELCHIOR, CASPAR, SERVANT:
(SIT)

ACT 3, SCENE 2 — *Parish Nativity Play*

HEROD: You heard what those men said! What does it mean? Where is this so-called saviour to be born?

ADVISER 1: Your Majesty is right to be concerned. The magi were correct in what they said. Our sacred texts, notably Isaiah, say that the birth will be in Bethlehem. Let me remind you what the scripture says: "Thou, Bethlehem in the land of Judah, are by no means least among Judah's kings, for out of thee there shall come a ruler born to shepherd my people, Israel."

HEROD: All that sham King David mythology.

ADVISER 2: Your Majesty, there is no need to be unduly alarmed by what you have heard. Although our scriptures speak of the Messiah, there is no process for confirming him. Our history is full of bogus claims by hotheads to be the true Messiah.

DIPLOMAT: But now, Your Majesty, we must face Rome which adds a layer of complexity.

HEROD: The Romans, being brutal, are well known for their policy of divide and rule. If they detect the tiniest dissent from my legitimate authority they will restore direct rule over us.

ADVISER 1: Your Majesty is absolutely right. We must allay confusion instantly.

Parish Nativity Play   ACT 3, SCENE 2

DIPLOMAT: Your Majesty, may I advise caution. These so-called wise men may assist our cause. Send them to Bethlehem so we may know without being present what has happened there, if anything; if not, then we are safe.

ADVISER 2: Encourage them, Your Majesty, to act on your behalf so that you may decide whether there is a need for drastic steps.

DIPLOMAT: Our scope for drastic action is curtailed, much better to rely on subtlety.

HEROD: A hint works for those who can take a hint but brutal minds require brutality.

DIPLOMAT: Truly, I sympathise, Your Majesty, but let us see what the wise men report before we contemplate brutality.

HEROD: I suppose so; I am resigned to wait until our guests return from Bethlehem. I think to allay fears I will advise the wise men of the course that they must take. Leave us alone now so that when we meet for dinner there is no controversy.

ADVISER 1, ADVISER 2, DIPLOMAT:
    (SIT)

BALTHASAR, MELCHIOR, CASPAR:
    (STAND)

ACT 3, SCENE 3 *Parish Nativity Play*

HEROD: I hope you are well settled, gentlemen. I am so pleased you came to visit me for advice on your way to Bethlehem. Go with my blessing. See what you can find. Search diligently for the new-born child. And when you find him, come and bring me word so that I may adore the Messiah.

BALTHASAR: We will be honoured to accept your charge. If we are right we will shortly return bringing good news of hope for Israel.

HEROD: Pray, take your couches, then I will take mine. (ASIDE)
The wise men are more certain in their views than my advisers, so I must prepare to take the drastic action which I deem essential to preserve my royal state; if that means death, my hand will not be stayed; this upstart must be killed immediately. These stubborn dogs can choke on their own blood if they oppose me as their common good.

SCENE 3: **An Inn in Bethlehem**
5 January 2 AD
INNKEEPER, SHEPHERD 1, SHEPHERD 2, STRANGER, SHEPHERD 3

INNKEEPER: You've never been in here so much before.

SHEPHERD 1: No wonder, our tale is still worth a drink!

SHEPHERD 2:	It's not wearing thin yet, but it soon will.
STRANGER:	I am newly arrived from Sephoris and, being alone, would enjoy a good yarn. I have heard many one- and two-drink tales but I see I must pay for three this time. My business has been good; I'll take the risk.
SHEPHERD 3:	I only have a small part to relate.
INNKEEPER:	There are no half drinks here, so pay for three.
STRANGER:	There's no need to be sharp. Here is your fee.
SCENE 4:	**Jacob's House, Bethlehem** **6 January 2 AD** JACOB, BALTHASAR, JOSEPH, MELCHIOR, CASPAR, ESTHER, MARY
JACOB:	You look bewildered, sirs; do you need help?
BALTHASAR:	Perhaps we do. We seek a special child born in this town, we think, quite recently, whose birth is indicated by a light you see now hovering above your head.
JACOB:	Ah yes! It has been here for many days above our house where there has been a birth.
BALTHASAR:	You say so! Was there anything special?
JACOB:	If you call angels special, why, then yes.

ACT 3, SCENE 4 *Parish Nativity Play*

BALTHASAR: Angels, you say? We certainly would count angels as special, do you not agree?

JACOB: But there have been so many recently.

JOSEPH: (STANDS)

JACOB: Here is the father of the holy child.

MELCHIOR: I am old now and never thought to live to see the day when such a child was born.

JOSEPH: I must admit I am a puzzled man. My wife, Mary, is much more comfortable. But if you have come here from afar, as your appearance surely indicates, how did you find us here so precisely?

CASPAR: The light up there has led us to the place. Its rising we foresaw a year ago!

JOSEPH: Remarkable! But everything is strange. Nothing is normal. We must learn to cope.

JACOB: Come in at once and take some bread with us. The boy will lead your camels to the inn.

BALTHASAR: One moment while we unload special gifts.

BALTHASAR, MELCHIOR, CASPAR:
(SIT)

JOSEPH: Where do you think our visitors come from?

Parish Nativity Play   ACT 3, SCENE 4

JACOB: Their complexions and clothes speak of strange parts: I fancy one from deepest Africa; one from the East; the third I cannot guess.

BALTHASAR, MELCHIOR, CASPAR, ESTHER:
(STAND)

JACOB: Welcome into my home. Here is my wife. Esther, these men have come from distant lands!

ESTHER: You are most welcome. Water, Miriam! Bake fresh bread and borrow a lamb for us!

MARY: (STANDS)

ESTHER: Here is my cousin Mary. I suppose her baby is the cause of your visit.

BALTHASAR: One only has to look to see the truth; her eyes are radiant with an inner light!

MARY: You are most welcome. I will bring the child.

BALTHASAR: We will do homage to him on behalf of all the world outside of Israel.

MARY: None but poor local shepherds have yet come, so you are first to represent the world.
(SITS)

JOSEPH: You have come very far. How were the roads?

ACT 3, SCENE 4 *Parish Nativity Play*

BALTHASAR: Given their treachery over Egypt, I find it hard to give the Romans praise but they have kept the peace these many years and there is nothing equal to their roads. There were unpleasant incidents, of course, mostly concerning cooks and innkeepers, the ordinary perils of strange lands when one is unaccustomed to the customs.

JACOB: But if you were so prescient of the light why did you come so late to Bethlehem?

MELCHIOR: We thought it right to call on King Herod who kept us for some days at his palace. He seemed reluctant to let us depart although he daily said the opposite.

JACOB: Choosing between the Romans and the King is like choosing between a hungry lion and a snake looking for innocent prey; I much prefer the lion, I must say.

JOSEPH: I hear my wife; please cause her no alarm.

MARY: (STANDS)
Here is the child the angel heralded, named Jeshua according to his word.

BALTHASAR: Let us all kneel and offer him our gifts.

Parish Nativity Play   ACT 3, SCENE 4

MELCHIOR: I, Melchior of Arabia, bring gold, the oldest treasure brought by me so old; my tribute fraught with untold suffering, offered in hope to a mysterious king; its slow accumulation soaked in blood, may it in your good hands only do good.

CASPAR: I, Caspar, King of Ethiopia, bring sweet frankincense as priestly offering; may it burn in the battle for the soul, where want and sacrifice make sinners whole; offered in awe to the Messiah priest who will be all, yet now appearing least.

BALTHASAR: I, Balthasar of Egypt, offer myrrh, the nemesis of the philosopher, for all must die, whatever they achieve; not even kings are granted a reprieve; yet the anointing with this special balm will save mankind from imperfection's harm.

JACOB: All spoken fairly; stand up now, I pray. We feel your thirst and hunger in ourselves.

ESTHER: Miriam! Are the lamb and bread prepared? Please take your ease. The food will soon arrive.

BALTHASAR: Now suddenly so dark, the light is gone! Yes, we will rest now that our work is done.

SCENE 5: **An Inn in Bethlehem**
6 January 2 AD
SHEPHERD 1, SHEPHERD 2, SHEPHERD 3, INNKEEPER

SHEPHERD 1: When I approached the man who just came in he said that he had heard our tale before.

SHEPHERD 2: The other who went out just before him said I was talking nonsense and left me.

SHEPHERD 3: I've seen it all before. People are fickle. Our luck has run its course; it's time to go.

INNKEEPER: Not until you have settled for three drinks. You might have seen a child born of a maid but you can't leave this place until you've paid!

SCENE 6: **Another Inn, Bethlehem, 6 January 2 AD**
BALTHASAR, GABRIEL

BALTHASAR: I am so restless that I hardly know if I am wide awake or fast asleep; seeing the child should have given me peace yet I am troubled, feeling turbulence.

GABRIEL: (STANDS)
Balthasar, Balthasar, be not afraid—that always seems to be my opening line—your worrying is highly justified; as you surmised, King Herod is a threat, vowing to do much more than you foresaw. He sees Jeshua as a competitor with ambitions to seize his tin-pot throne, resolved to kill him with the news you bring. Already worried at your slow return, he plans to capture and imprison you under the guise of hospitality. Do not return to Alexandria together, making apprehension swift, but travel each directly to his home; a convoy will play into Herod's hands.

BALTHASAR: A dream or not, this is a safe command. Who will save Jeshua from Herod's hand?

GABRIEL: Scripture demands that Jeshua, the first son, be offered by his parents to the Lord. He will be safe till then, but afterwards I will warn Joseph, so that he may flee before King Herod reacts violently.

SCENE 7: **The Temple in Jerusalem**
2 February 2 AD
ANNA, SIMEON, JOSEPH, MARY

ANNA: Father Simeon, pray, are you unwell?

ACT 3, SCENE 7 — *Parish Nativity Play*

SIMEON: A strange day, Anna, so I might look strange. Today will be the last day of my life, not because I am unwell but because the time I have been waiting for has come. The Holy Spirit came to me last night saying that what I have believed is true, that I will not die until I have seen Israel's consolation, born for us, and God's gift through Israel to all the world. That day has come, my greatest yet my last.

ANNA: Happy yet sad news, holy Simeon! If this is so, I will be ready, too. My sojourn here will not have been in vain. For more than sixty years since I mourned I have prayed for this day unceasingly.

ANNA: (SITS)

JOSEPH, MARY: (STAND)

JOSEPH: I wish it had been more; I feel ashamed and yet two doves are all we can afford.

MARY: Joseph, there is no need to be ashamed: in offering our first-born to the Lord we far exceed an animal sacrifice.

JOSEPH: Mary, properly said, I am rebuked.

MARY: I did not mean to chide you, Joseph dear.

SIMEON: The Lord's Messiah! Alleluia!

MARY: Pray, holy father! Take my holy child!

SIMEON:	Lord, let your servant now depart in peace according to your word; such sweet release! For I have seen salvation in this face for Israel and all the human race; glory of Israel, answer to our call, light to the Gentiles, come to save us all.
JOSEPH:	The Spirit must have moved you to such thoughts.
MARY:	O wonder at such words—I am amazed; pray, bless my son and us. The Lord be praised.
SIMEON:	All blessing given to me I gladly give to him whose promise has kept me alive. This child is destined for the rise and fall of many in divided Israel. His words will touch the hearts of those who pray, and bring relief to sheep which go astray. Goodness which leads some sinners to repent, yet hardens others who will not relent. A sword will pierce your soul for you will see your son killed by Temple authority.
ANNA:	(STANDS) Praise to the child, all here who believe in God's promise of Israel's reprieve. Look, see the child, Messiah for us all; renounce your evil ways and hear his call.
JOSEPH:	Now come, Mary, the turmoil is too great.
MARY:	Yes, Joseph, now I wish to be apart, to store both curse and blessing in my heart.

ACT 3, SCENE 8 — *Parish Nativity Play*

SCENE 8: **King Herod's Palace, Jerusalem**
3 February 2 AD
HEROD, ADVISER 1, ADVISER 2

HEROD: Those three magi have made a fool of me, seen through my ruse to find the 'royal child' to put a stop to war and anarchy. I should have known those oily Easterners would slide out of my grasp. What shall I do?

ADVISER 1: May I counsel caution, Your Majesty? Attaching blame without sound evidence is unwise. There may be good reasons why the men have not returned. It may be that they could not find the child in Bethlehem or found him and thought that they were misled. It may amount to nothing after all.

ADVISER 2: Prevention out-ranks cure, Your Majesty! The Romans like decisiveness in kings. You never know what the child presages. Only yesterday in the Temple Court our spies reported unrest in the crowd, centred upon a child thought to be great. It passed off quickly, but you never know.

HEROD: Counsels of caution are unfit for kings who must survive by fear, not gentleness. Send my best soldiers down to Bethlehem to kill all boys below the age of two. What cunning cannot solve, violence must do.

SCENE 9: **An Inn, Jerusalem**
3 February 2 AD
JOSEPH, GABRIEL

JOSEPH: More than six weeks have passed since we left home. Time to return to family and work. I never have much liked Jerusalem; it fills me with fear I cannot explain.

GABRIEL: (STANDS) Quite right, Joseph, you have reason to fear. King Herod seeks to murder your new son, so you must flee to Egypt instantly.

JOSEPH: To Egypt where our ancestors were slaves?

GABRIEL: I understand your sense of irony but Egypt is the nearest place of safety. Then in four years return to Galilee when Herod and Archelaus are both dead.

JOSEPH: The burden is too much for me to bear. I lack the strength that Mary has displayed. It was she that consented and not me.

GABRIEL: Patience, Joseph, God's grace is limitless; but salvation is freighted with distress.

SCENE 10: **The Temple Court, Jerusalem**
1 April 12 AD
JOSEPH, MARY, JESHUA, ELDER 1, ELDER 2

JOSEPH: (PAUSE)
Three days of searching in Jerusalem have brought no hope of finding Jeshua. When we could not find him among our folk perhaps we were wrong to retrace our steps; he might be lying dead along the road! After eight quiet years since we came home we find ourselves again in deep distress.

MARY: I too am worried, but yet reassured by what Simeon said about the boy. His purpose cannot be attained through death at such a tender age. He is alive. Strange that his future death can reassure.

JOSEPH: We have searched every alleyway and street. Here is the Temple courtyard; let us pray.

MARY: We should have come here first to offer prayers instead of scurrying about Jerusalem. Look for a quiet corner, Joseph dear.

JESHUA, ELDER 1, ELDER 2:
(STAND)

JESHUA: It is not that love is above the law. Love, not the law, will set God's people free. Love is, you see, intrinsic to the law. The gleaning rules in Deuteronomy and all commandments clarify the case, not demanding conditionality but unlimited giving forth in grace. What was intended, by my Father's will which all his chosen people must embrace in giving, was the power to fulfil his purpose in responsibility for each other, in times of good and ill: unbounded love, not reciprocity. The only contract which the law permits, to which your position stands contrary, is our faith in return for benefits which God has promised. He will keep his word. Among us, and not on a throne he sits.

ELDER 1: For one so young you are too confident, doubting the wisdom of a thousand years.

ELDER 2: Yet he recites his Torah well enough!

ELDER 1: Knowing the words and knowing what they mean are different. He should proceed with care.

JOSEPH: What, you here, Jeshua! Where have you been? Forgive my interruption, learned sirs; I thought my child whom you see here was lost.

ACT 3, SCENE 10   Parish Nativity Play

ELDER 1:   He has been with us for the last three days. I never heard a child more confident. He is a credit to his upbringing, although he lacks a proper reverence for his elders and what they represent.

JESHUA: Respected teachers, do not be afraid! My Father gave us brains to understand. He will be with us if he is obeyed.

MARY: My child, why have you treated us this way? See how you have caused such anxiety. For three days we have been searching for you.

JESHUA: Oh sweet mother! Why did you search for me? You know that I am safe from human snares. Now that I am a man do you not see that I must care for my Father's affairs, where love outranks barren theology, mingling holy learning with my prayers?

MARY: We do not understand, but why should we? We did not expect ease. Let us depart. I will treasure your sayings in my heart.

JESHUA: Fathers, farewell! Now it is time to go to feed on holy writ and simple bread; I need some years to pray and think and grow before I set out in my Father's stead to give my life for all that he has said.

EPILOGUE: **Heaven**
15 April 12 AD

HOLY SPIRIT

HOLY SPIRIT: Those from which I eternally proceed have, with my grace, accomplished what we willed: the heavenly word incarnate in the deed, the promise of old covenants fulfilled, not by an edict but in human guise, yet still with all our attributes instilled. Our play has shown this heavenly surprise bringing new hope where there had been despair, a shining promise in a baby's eyes, not only for Judea but everywhere, the chance to love in greater harmony, not freed from but embracing human care, bound by our love in solidarity, made concrete in the birth of Mary's son, a deed more faithful than philosophy. The word made flesh, our drama now is done, man by this Incarnation is set free to love, but the great prize is not yet won: how bittersweet his story yet will be from crib to cross, Bethlehem to Calvary!

EU GPSR Authorized Representative:

LOGOS EUROPE, 9 rue Nicolas Poussin, 17000 La Rochelle, France

contact@logoseurope.eu

www.ingramcontent.com/pod-product-compliance
Lightning Source LLC
Chambersburg PA
CBHW050555160426
43199CB00015B/2669